B.A.

FIELD TRIPS

The Zoo

Stuart A. Kallen
ABDO & Daughters

Published by Abdo & Daughters, 4940 Viking Drive, Suite 622, Edina, Minnesota 55435.

Printed in the United States.

Cover and Interior Photo credits: Peter Arnold, Inc.
                                   Archive Photos
                                   Wide World Photos
Illustration: Ben Dann Lander
Edited by Julie Berg

Library of Congress Cataloging-in-Publication Data

Kallen, Stuart A., 1955-
The zoo / Stuart A. Kallen.
      p.   cm. — (Field trips)
Includes index.
Summary: Discusses zoos, their purposes, the people who work there, and the animals who may be found there.
ISBN 1-56239-712-5
1. Zoos—Juvenile literature. 2. Zoo animals—Juvenile literature. [1. Zoos. 2. Zoo animals.]
I. Title. II. Series.
QL76.K34 1997
590'.74'4—dc20   96-18870
                                                      CIP
                                                       AC

Contents

Lions and Tigers and Bears!

It's a wild world full of millions of animals. Snakes and bats and birds and monkeys roam the Earth. Some animals live far away in Africa or China. Some live right in your back yard.

Animals live in the mountains and deserts. Animals live in the ocean. Some animals live in **grasslands**. And every animal needs certain foods to stay alive. The place an animal lives is called its **habitat**. An animal's habitat gives it everything it needs to survive.

But not all animals live in their own habitats. Some of them are world travelers. They live in places called zoos. Zoos are collections of animals from all over the world. The job of a zoo is to give animals habitats like their homes in the wild. That's why zoos are so much fun to visit. And such hard work for the people who run them.

This zoo provides a habitat for these black-footed penguins.

Visit the Zoo

When you walk into a zoo, your senses come alive. New sights, smells, and sounds are everywhere. There are shops with toy animals and T-shirts. There are huge pools with sea animals. And there are hundreds of animals everywhere.

Where do you begin? Usually signs will point the way to different displays. You can visit your favorite animals first, or save them until the end. Maybe the sea animals will be putting on a show.

Opposite page: Visitors inside a hummingbird aviary at the San Diego Zoo.

6

Zookeepers

Visitors to a zoo have a lot of fun. But caring for the animals in a zoo is hard work. You'll see **zookeepers** who do this work. Zoo workers are usually dressed in rubber boots and overalls. They carry brooms, hoses, and shovels to clean the animal's living areas.

Zookeepers also feed and care for animals. They watch an animal's weight and diet to make sure the animal is staying healthy. If an animal is sick, the keeper will bring in an animal doctor called a **veterinarian**. Vets give animals regular checkups, shots, and other care.

You might learn about animals from a zookeeper. They teach lessons and answer any questions you might have.

Opposite page: This zookeeper bottle-feeds a month-old walrus.

9

Eating Like a Bunch of Animals

You'll see a lot of animals eating. Every animal needs a different kind of food. Zoos must buy more kinds of food than a restaurant. Keepers feed animals fruits, eggs, hay, vegetables, sunflower seeds, peanuts, worms, meat, grain, pet chow, vitamins, and minerals.

Every animal's needs are different. Baby animals need special diets. Some animals like to eat alone. Others eat in groups. Some eat different foods as the seasons change. When you see animals munching, notice what they're eating. Are they alone? Or do they eat together?

Vampire bats must drink one cup of fresh animal blood every day! And one elephant eats 600 pounds (272 kg) of food. Ask a **zookeeper** what your favorite animal eats.

Opposite page: Baby elephants gorge on pineapples, bananas and sugar cane.

Every day **zookeepers** serve animals foods that are raw, cooked, ground, diced, sliced, served live, hot, cold, or mixed in a stew. When visitors feed animals in a zoo, it may hurt the animal. Never throw food to animals in a zoo. Does all this make you hungry? Most zoos have restaurants where you can eat.

Petting zoo

NURSERY

BUG WOR

Animal Habitat

Just as each animal needs different food, each animal needs a different **habitat**. In the wild, animals run, swim, and fly. In a zoo, they must stay in a small area. That is why zoos try to make animal homes as nice as possible.

Zoos design animal living areas to be like their natural habitat. Some zoos have buildings that are like jungles or **rain forests**. Other areas are like deserts or **grasslands**. Birds live in giant bird houses called **aviaries**. Dolphins, seals, and fish need huge pools of water to swim in. Sometimes zoos put a pane of glass into a dolphin tank so visitors can watch them swim.

The Toronto Zoo in Canada has a train that takes visitors through wooded areas where bears and bison live. The Frankfurt Zoo in Germany has a crocodile jungle.

Opposite page: This river otter lives in a swamp built by the Brookfield Zoo.

Living Like Animals

Just like people, some animals are shy. Some are show-offs. And some like to sleep all day. Zoos must give every animal what it needs to be happy. You'll see animals playing and sleeping. Some just like to act silly.

Sometimes male and female animals must be kept apart because they don't live together in the wild. Antelopes are shy and need peace and quiet. Otters like to swim all day and sleep somewhere warm. **Reptiles**, like snakes, need a warm place and plenty of sunshine or heat lights.

Opposite page: Chimpanzees like to group together. The zoo must provide a place for them to hang around.

Baby Animals

Many zoos have areas where only baby animals live. This is called the "petting zoo." That means you can pet and touch the baby animals. But be nice. Those animals get petted all day. They like to be treated gently.

A langur and its baby.

The first purebred
Rothschild giraffe
born at the Perth
Zoo in Western
Australia. The tall
male baby is seen
being kissed by its
mother on its first
public outing
at the zoo.

New Kinds of Zoos

Some people think it's cruel to keep animals in a cage. To solve that problem, new kinds of zoos are being built. In these new zoos, animals can roam free over a large area while people drive through in their cars. These kinds of zoos are called wildlife parks.

At one zoo in Hawaii, a mechanical toy squirrel jumps around for the tigers to play with. At the Brookfield Zoo in Chicago, sand cats hunt live insects. At the Miami Monkey Jungle visitors walk through paths covered with netting while the monkeys move around freely. There, it's people who are in the cages!

Now that you are familiar with what goes on at a zoo, visiting one will be a lot more fun!

Opposite page: Lions sleeping in a wildlife park in Kenya, Africa.

Glossary

aviary (AY-vee-air-ee) - a large building where birds are kept.

extinct (ek-STINKT) - to no longer be alive.

grassland - an area where many types of grasses grow.

habitat (HAB-uh-tat) - the natural living space of a plant or animal.

rain forest - a tropical forest with a high yearly rainfall— also known as jungles.

reptile - a cold-blooded animal with scales such as a turtle, lizard, or snake.

veterinarian (vet-uh-NAIR-ee-an) - an animal doctor.

zookeeper - a person who works at a zoo.

Index